YOU
ALREADY
KNOW
THIS
TOO

Original
Inspiration
PUBLISHING

OriginalInspirationPublishing.com

YOU
ALREADY
KNOW
THIS
TOO

Heather M. Clarke

Original
Inspiration
P U B L I S H I N G

ISBN 978-0-9988038-3-8

Published by Original Inspiration Publishing
Arizona, USA

I dedicate this book to my sweet Ed who crossed over recently. I could not have had a better husband. Sorry about that, everyone else. I know you think your husband is pretty awesome, but Ed beat him out by a mile.

He would do anything for me if I asked him. He was totally supportive of whatever I wanted to do. He gave me all the space I needed during all of our 50 years of marriage. He was my rock.

When we went to Costa Rica back in 2003, Sonia Choquette recognized how powerful he was, and she told me he was like a container for me… holding the space for me as I bounced all over the place, absorbing a lot of negative energy that was coming at me.

Ed has been my best friend for 51 years. He was a very wise old soul, and I have been blessed to have shared my life with him for so long.

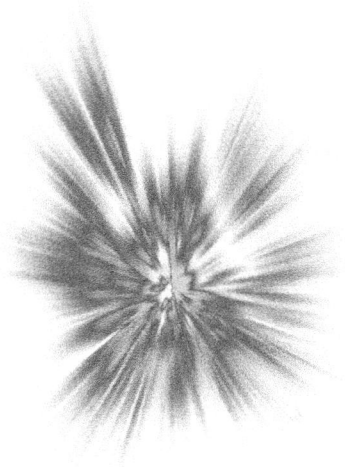

WHAT PEOPLE HAVE SAID ABOUT VOL I:

I can't express enough how much I am enjoying your book! Short, informative, funny, interesting, leaving me anxious to read on! I hope to see other volumes from you. Perfect title too... thanks for putting yourself out there! — S. I., Phoenix, Arizona

Your book helped me through a month of problems. I live close to where the hurricane hit. Even though I wasn't in the path, I still got heavy rains and lost power for 24 hrs. Because of the storm, I went a few days without work and with no way to hear from the outside world, so I reread parts of your book. I put some of what you said into what I was going through and before I knew it, everything was almost back to normal. — C. K., Baton Rouge, Louisiana

I want you to know how much I've enjoyed your book. I've been reading a story or so to my husband at night before going to sleep. I think it's been "meat" that he has really grabbed onto in his journey. While I recognize many of your teachings (I, too, am a student of the Course), I love your contextual stories. Thank you for publishing it! — J. R, Litchfield Park, Arizona

After meals, I kick my legs up on the table and read aloud to my husband. So many outright laughs and appreciation of bringing you right up to our kitchen table. I began reading the story of your dog Bud and your greatest fear of having to put him down. I got to the part where you heard Bud speaking to you. Even before I could speak his words, I felt I had walked into this wall of vast emotion. I was immediately stopped in my tracks. I was overfilled with emotion; my heart feeling like it couldn't move; I couldn't breathe. I needed time to collect myself. One minute I was there; the next I was completely somewhere else. I eventually got through the story and only felt relief when Bud crossed over. I was very happy for him. — K. R., British Columbia

CONTENTS

PREFACE

The experience of writing a book is quite fascinating. I wrote Volume I of this series pretty much behind the scenes, without telling any of my friends I was doing it. It came together so easily as soon as I was willing to sit down and get on with it. Once I got the guidance about how to set it up as a collection of short, two-page-maximum stories, I had no more blocks to getting started.

When I finally had the copies of Volume I in my hands, I started talking to everyone about it. As I share how it all came about, what I see is that my experience is actually turning on the pilot light in many of my friends who are *also* getting messages to *write the book*. We all have amazing stories, knowledge and inspiration to share, and it is *time* to get it written down and disseminated throughout the world.

I sent a book to my cousin who is in prison in Louisiana, and he shared it with the chaplain. The chaplain immediately ordered three copies. One day, Breck saw someone walking down the hall, carrying a copy. Then a couple of weeks later, he walked into a college class he was taking, and there was a copy of the book on the teacher's desk! She started the class that day reading the story entitled "You Can Have Any Outcome You Choose." After class, Breck took his copy and a picture of me to show the teacher. She had no idea he was related to the author.

Another time, we were in our Course in Miracles class and Clydene, a member of our group, shared that she had a friend who had two dogs, one of which was *really* old and decrepit. Clydene read the story to her friend about my taking my dog in to be put down. Right after that, the friend was able to take her precious pet in to be put to sleep and was completely at peace about it.

Stories like this give me such gratification for having finally written the book and getting it out to as many people as I can. I sincerely hope something I have written will make a difference in your life.

Heather M. Clarke

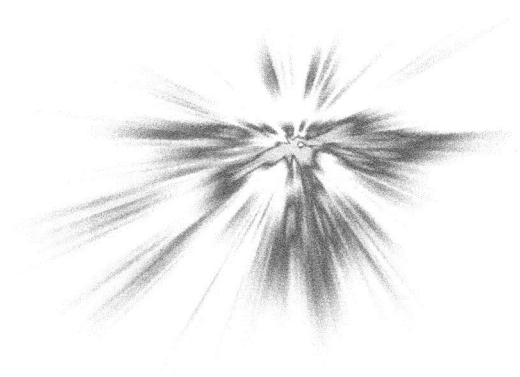

INTRODUCTION

For years, I have had a Voice inside me, dropping hints I should write a book. My problem—my excuse—is I have SO much to write about, I don't know where to start… so, of course, I don't start. Then once during a class, the Voice interrupted my thoughts and said, "Don't sit down to write a book. Sit down to write a chapter. Or sit down to write just one page." I then realized all I needed to do was to get some paper, my favorite pen, and *start*. I decided to think of it as writing a series of essays on different subjects.

When I get these kinds of ideas, it's like having a "bee in my bonnet," and I have to do something about it *now*. I write in journals all the time. I have one in the car, one in the bathroom, one in my purse, one in my bedroom. When an idea pops in, I absolutely have to get it on paper.

It's like always having a friend with me who is ready to listen to whatever is on my mind—and she never interrupts me, unless it is my Inner Voice interrupting to give me some new gem of wisdom.

You have a similar Inner Voice. Start writing out your thoughts when you are upset about something or feel some inspiration popping up. You will surprise yourself to read all the wisdom flowing out on the paper. Are you willing to give it a try?

HEY, DON'T CALL ME A WIDOW!

I am a Surviving Spouse

When I wrote Volume I of this series, my husband Ed was going through the advanced stages of Parkinson's Disease and dementia. On the Sunday after Thanksgiving in 2017, he finally released that tired, old worn-out body.

I was very fortunate to have had more than three years' notice he was leaving so I could get myself prepared mentally to be without him. Since our mother died suddenly of a brain hemorrhage one night in 1990, we know what a shock it is to a family when someone dies with no warning. He used to ask me how was I going to handle my financial situation. What would I do if he dropped dead right there on the kitchen floor? Who should I call, a funeral home or 911? Did I have his funeral planned?

I felt he was like the front desk secretary at an elementary school who had been there for 35 years. She knew you and your kids by name. Everyone loved her. She gave notice in September that she would be retiring at the end of the year. That gave everyone time to say goodbye and be ready for someone else to be at her desk next year. She was done and ready for her next adventure.

Now I am in the period of transitioning into being single. It takes me about three weeks to fill up the recycle bin to put it out front. Those huge garbage bins would take me a month! But I finally realized I don't have to fill it all the way up before I can take it out! I am always washing a small load of clothes rather than a medium or large. I run the dishwasher maybe once a week. I gauge how old something is by whether we got it before or after he passed. I found two little frozen entrees in the freezer that were specifically for him, so they have to be over 18 months old! It is like dates that are BC or AD…we have BE and AE, "Before Ed" and "After Ed."

Even though he is "gone." I feel like he is very close here in the house. I often get messages from him through several of my intuitive friends, and I know he has been very busy taking care of some issues in the family, helping to arrange the manifestation of the Arizona Enlightenment Center, and watching over all of us.

BOTTOM LINE:
What makes you feel better, to call yourself a widow or a surviving spouse? Surviving spouse sounds to me like it is still full of life. That's what I choose.

WHAT ARE YOU PASSIONATE ABOUT?

*You play a big part in raising the vibration
of the planet by just being peaceful.*

Make a list of all the things you could be passionate about—your family, your country, your career, your kids, your spouse, your education. How about your team? What could bring up more passion than a well-played NBA game that is tied with 1.8 seconds left and a guy off the bench—not one of the superstars—hits his first game-winning basket for *your* team? Winning is much more fun than losing.

I am passionate about learning stuff. I love to go to workshops, lectures, classes, and seminars to learn something new. When our son Dan went to Northern Arizona University, Ed and I took him up there for the Orientation Weekend. I get excited being on a college campus because all the students there are taking the classes needed to get them prepared for their life path. I told Ed we should check into the married students' dorm and take every class the university offered that interested us.

But after giving it more thought, I realized my biggest passion is for life itself. I love to experience all kinds of different events and places. I love to be with people who are also passionate about life. I love to spontaneously go out to dinner with my neighbors with only a three-minute notice. I love to lay around all day reading an intriguing new book. I love to stay up till 2 am and be able to sleep till 10 in the morning if I want to. I love to go to a Deva Premal concert and cry because the music is soooo unbelievably beautiful. I LOVE the deep vibration of drums!

Have you noticed lately that events are moving at the speed of thought? People all over the world are waking up spiritually and then connecting with other awakened people, and everyone is filled with this growing feeling of anticipation—that something huge is about to happen and we get to be a part of it.

Yes, there probably will always be wars and conflict going on somewhere in the world, but you can choose whether to focus on that or on what is positive. Offer your peace of mind to every situation you find yourself in.

BOTTOM LINE:
You have a big influence on what is going on here.
What can you do to make this day unforgettable?

STOP ARGUING WITH WHAT IS

We spend a lot of time expecting people to be someone other than who they are.

Byron Katie wrote a powerful book called *Loving What Is*. I highly recommend it. It will take a lot of the stress and frustration out of your life from being irritated when someone you know keeps doing the same annoying thing over and over.

We have lived in Phoenix off and on since 1965. We think it is funny how the heat is such a big topic of conversation. It is hot here in the summer. It just is. It does it every year. Never fails. So let's just move on. We will not be able to change it. I often say it isn't so bad as long as you don't have to work outside. I really feel for landscapers and roofers. They start work as soon as it is light enough so they can be done by noon when it starts to really heat up. Imagine how stressful it would be to be homeless here in the summer! (Of course, it would be stressful to be homeless, period!)

So—who is doing something habitually in your life that is driving you absolutely nuts? Your teenage son who leaves the toilet seat up every time, in spite of your constant nagging? Your mother who interrupts you and fills in the end of your sentence every time you get together? If you want to get rid of some unnecessary stress from your life, it is time to make a shift and choose another way to look at the issue. The fact is, your mother has always interrupted you, and she probably will continue. Accept that "flaw" and accept her the way she is. If your son leaves the toilet seat up, you have a few choices: continue to be irritated that he does not hear you, ignore it and leave the seat up, or put it down yourself. What will bring you the most peace? The main goal is for *you* to feel good.

Our expectations can cause a lot of conflict in our lives. The truth is—this is who I am. This is who your husband is. This is who your friend is. It just IS—accept everyone (and yourself) for who he or she is and relax. It is not your job to change everybody.

BOTTOM LINE:
YOU are your only project.

THANK HEAVENS FOR FLUSH TOILETS!

Live your life from a place of gratitude.

Can you imagine living in a home or community with no running water or flush toilets? We are so spoiled and take so many things for granted. Flush toilets are a *major* plus in our lives! It is easy to slip into being irritable and judgmental and negative about aspects of our lives. Pay attention! Just quit it! (Easier said than done, no?)

I remember when I was in elementary school, I felt so privileged I had been put into a family with a mother who for some reason knew all the right brands of food to buy! What a blessing! She bought Bosco Chocolate Syrup, Heinz Ketchup, Miracle Whip, Velveeta Cheese, Wonder Bread, Cheerios, Buicks. How did I luck out so much?

Can you look at your body and thank it for supporting you, even if it is not perfect? Thank your feet for getting you everywhere you need to go. Your lungs keep bringing in the oxygen. Your heart keeps beating. (When I was young, I visualized a big, strong, bald guy sitting in the center of my chest, slamming his huge hammer on a big rock, creating the constant rhythm of my beating heart. I always thought I would stay alive as long as he kept beating that rock.)

I had a somewhat trying day a couple months ago and as I was driving home, I just craved a Coke. I only have a Pepsi or Coke two or three times a year, but sometimes, I simply have to have one. It took a while to find a fast food place. As I was driving, I did a great job of overcoming all of the reasons I should *not* get one. I succeeded, but when I pulled up to the drive-through window, I did compromise and order a kid's size. I have to say that was the best Coke ever! Absolutely perfect fizziness, perfect size, perfect sweetness, perfect coldness. It was awesome! I am still grateful to have had that experience!

As I drive down my street, there are a few houses that are not exactly well maintained, so there can be weeds, junk piled in the yard, ridiculous colors of paint (in my opinion—the owner loves them), dead trees, too many cars, etc., etc. Now, I can focus on those irritants, or I can choose to see what really does look nice. Some people have remodeled so their homes are beautiful, some people love flowers and have magnificent gardens, some people have a pristine yard with not even one weed. What makes me feel better, the irritants or the beauty? Why would I focus on the irritants? How does that serve me?

BOTTOM LINE:
I make it a great day by being grateful for everything.

THIS HAPPENED, AND THAT HAPPENED, AND THIS HAPPENED, THEN…

OK, OK, it's time for me to commit to getting outside and walking!

Do you recognize when you are being guided from one place and experience to another? I just realized that is going on in my life now.

I have prided myself on being 73 and basically not having a doctor. I go to naturopathic doctors and intuitive healers occasionally, and I have not been to an "RD" (Regular Doctor) since 2012. I am very proud I don't have any diagnosis other than a mild case of rosacea on my face that pops up every once in a while.

About a month ago, I started taking CBD oil every day that is really helping me sleep better. However, soon I developed a urinary tract infection. I am aware that CBD oil detoxifies your body, so I possibly could have had a low-grade infection hanging out for a long time and the oil just brought it to the surface. This required me to go to an Urgent Care clinic to be tested. This led me to have to connect with an "RD" for a follow up after I finished the antibiotic.

Since I had not had a regular physical for seven years, I decided to go back to the doctor I had gone to way back then and get some testing done. I had a mammogram, full blood tests, and a DEXA scan for bone density.

Turns out the DEXA scan showed I have symptoms of a condition of the bones that starts with an "O." (I am not willing to "own" the diagnosis!) And then I went back to the doctor for a follow up to learn what I needed to do about it.

Just look at everything that lined up to get me to a doctor to find out I have something I need to take care of. I am not freaking out about it. I am just definitely willing to make some lifestyle changes. I hardly ever do any exercising, and now I am committed to going outside every day to walk and getting some Vitamin D naturally from sunshine and taking some bone-building supplements.

Look around and see how your Guides are orchestrating the circumstances in your life to align you with the most benevolent outcome for your highest and best interest.

BOTTOM LINE:
You are in good hands.

WE ALL NEED
A BEST FRIEND

Or do we?

Some days I wake up feeling funky. I don't like it. It is cloudy and rainy and I am kinda bouncing around the house from one organizing task to another.

I just realized I lost my best friend of 51 years when my husband died. I can't believe it took so long to sink in. Yet, even though I miss him, I can feel his presence here in the house, and I never feel alone or lonely. It just dawned on me that you need a best friend to go with you to experience all the beauty and joy in the world. When you see something amazing, like one of our exquisite Arizona sunsets, you want to share it with someone.

Interestingly, Marilyn Harper, the speaker at our weekly group, just "happened" to talk about this. This is actually an opportunity for *me* to spend some time with me without feeling like I am not complete. She reminded us that *we* are our own best friend. We are complete already and don't need to have anyone else around to make us whole. So, this is just my chance to experience *myself.* I can have all kinds of adventures either on my own or with a few of my friends. I get to have it both ways!

We are lucky we have so few cloudy, "funky" days here in Arizona. The sun is out almost all the time. We actually like a cloudy day occasionally, just because it is a change from the constant sunny, clear days. However, give us three rainy or overcast days in a row, and we start to forget what the sun looks like. We are not happy about it.

Do you keep yourself busy with all kinds of unnecessary tasks to help the time pass? Can you stand to be alone with yourself? You really are a unique individual. Get to know yourself! Work to have a good mix of time with other people and time with yourself.

If you get affected by gloomy weather, you can use the experience as a time to step back and spend a little time reflecting about what is going on. What can this teach you? How can you see it another way so you don't let yourself get bogged down? Get out your journal and write some messages from your Guides to give you some insight about this stage of life. You might just amaze yourself. I did that myself today, and this is what I wrote:

You are so not alone. Sometimes you have to just step back and take a breath. Learn how to be with yourself. We will bring who you need to team up with later when the time is right. WE are with you now.

Pretty comforting.

BOTTOM LINE:
Being alone does not mean being lonely.

I NEED CREDENTIALS!

I need to feel legitimate.

Many people have a "need" to get more and more training so they can have all those letters after their name, such as BS, MA, PhD, etc. You probably have come across business cards of a couple people you know who have a complete alphabet soup after their name. It seems like they can't stop taking more classes to get yet another certification.

When I was working in disaster relief with the Red Cross, I dealt with a lot of people who had just lost their homes and sometimes their pets and even their children. I felt like I needed more training than I was getting through the Red Cross to be able to help them. I signed up for a class at the University of Phoenix that would lead to my receiving a master's degree in psychology. We had to take a 3-week course before we were accepted into the program where we had to give a seven-minute talk and write a ten-page paper on what aspect of psychology we wanted to focus on—and it could not be "private practice." We had to show we were capable of handling master's-level classes. The instructor was like a drill sergeant as he described the assignments. He directed us to not get up in front of the class and get all emotional about something and start crying. He said, "We are not Oprah here!"

As I was working on what I would talk and write about, I realized I did not want to focus on alcoholics, battered women, and abused children. I *do* relate to Oprah, and I want to help people feel better, raise their vibration, and realize their potential. I wanted to be in the position to be an "up-lifter." After only one class in the $300 three-week preparation course, I decided not to continue because I wanted to invest most of my time being involved with people who are excited, happy, and ready to make a difference in the world. I dropped out, unable to get a refund, but I realized I was able to let go of the need to have the MA listed after my name on my business card. It let me get that out of my system!

My teacher, Dr. Joseph Dillard, addressed this in one of our classes a few years back. He realized many people felt the need to have several degrees to make themselves feel "complete." He pointed out that Jesus did not have a single degree listed after his name, and he seemed to make quite an impact on the world. That is such a great reminder for me to recognize I am complete just as I am today. (I did notice, though, that Dr. Dillard *does* have the PhD letters after his name! Ha!)

***

BOTTOM LINE:
Nothing is lacking or missing in my life.

IS THAT REALLY A COINCIDENCE?

Everything that happens to us
happens for our good.

In 2003, Ed and I attended a retreat in Costa Rica presented by Sonia Choquette. There were 24 of us in the group. It was a life-changing experience. One evening as we were walking to the dining hall for dinner, I was on the phone trying to handle a problem with an appraisal that came in *$50,000* low on a house I had sold just before we left. Ed was walking ahead, talking with Connie, a woman from Connecticut. She asked him what he did in life as his career, and he said that he had been in the Air Force for twenty years before going into selling real estate for another twenty years. She mentioned she used to date a guy in the Air Force. Ed asked what his name was—as if he would have any chance of knowing the one Air Force person she had dated. She replied that his name was John McFalls. Ed just about fell over! That just happens to be my BROTHER!! Wow! It turned out she knew my mother, my sister and my grandmother!

Our son Dan went to college at Northern Arizona University in Flagstaff, earning a degree in Computer Science and Engineering. He decided he wanted to be a video game programmer after he graduated, so he got busy sending out resumes and applications for an internship at any company he could find. He wanted to attend a Computer Gaming Conference in Santa Clara that summer, so we paid the registration fee as a graduation present. When he got to the conference by himself, he felt quite overwhelmed with the whole thing—especially the job fair. On the last day, he picked up some lunch and sat down in the lobby to eat. Soon, a guy came over and asked if he could join him. As they started making small talk, Dan mentioned he had applied for an internship at Quicksilver in Long Beach—and it "just happened" that the guy sitting there was from Quicksilver and had actually seen his application! Dan ended up getting hired for the internship and has continued as a full-time programmer ever since. Now, if he had attended the conference with a friend, that connection possibly would never have happened. That guy most likely would not have joined him for lunch.

We have a spiritual group that meets every Wednesday morning at a local church. People get drawn to this group and don't even know how it happened. Darlene had been in the group for a couple years when Susan came for the first time. Darlene immediately recognized her from Washington State where they had both lived. Susan had done a group healing session that completely changed Darlene's life. Darlene lost track of her and had been looking for her for years to thank her…and one day, she walked into our group in Surprise, Arizona!

BOTTOM LINE:
Your Guides are very busy arranging all the circumstances in your life for your next step. Isn't it fun?

THE BAG OF ICE

*Stay alert as to how other people
are affecting you.*

Every one of us has an effect on our community. What happens to one of us ripples out to affect everyone else. A great way to demonstrate this is to look at what happens when you pull a bag of ice out of the freezer. Sometimes it can be a solid block, and you will have to break it up to be able to use it. When you slam it on the floor of your kitchen, suddenly all the cubes separate and become individuals. When you put a lot of pressure on a community that is close-minded and holding solid with one particular viewpoint, the pressure (being slammed on the floor) breaks up the block, allowing a community of individual ideas to break loose. *Everybody* affects everybody else. *Every action* affects the community. Are you adding to the experience in a positive way, or are you stirring the pot and adding conflict?

I am active in two very inspirational meetings every week where I get to interact with up to 50-60 people. Many of them come up to me after the meeting and thank me for facilitating them, and I always tell them the meetings would not be so powerful and life-changing if no one showed up. Each person is a vital part of the whole community, and the attendance of every one of them is essential to make that meeting so significant. You are *all* an important piece of the puzzle, so when you wake up and decide to attend, recognize you are contributing to the experience of every one else in the group.

We affect people who come across our path every day. We either say something that helps wake them up, or they say something to help shift us. Remember the candle-lighting ceremonies at church on Christmas Eve? One person lights the first person's candle and that person lights the next person's candle and that person lights the next one. It goes on until every candle in the room has been lit up. The light expands and expands. Every time you say some words of wisdom to someone, you have lit that candle and that person can go out and say something that helps someone else.

Your ego does not want you to know how powerful you are. You can help people release their grief and fear. You can help heal the world. You ignite the divine spark in everyone you meet.

This is Pay-It-Forward: You have been affected and transformed by the words your teachers have used. Now *you* will become the teacher, and your "students" will be transformed and be able to go out and pass it on to others.

～◦◦◦◦◦◦◦～

BOTTOM LINE:
Don't give anyone the power to affect
your life in a negative way.

IT'S TIME TO PUT UP SOME BOUNDARIES

You are not required to let anyone consume your every free moment.

It is easy to get bogged down in trying to help people. You want to be compassionate and helpful, but it is essential for you to set some boundaries to be compassionate and helpful to *you*.

I am sure you have had or currently have someone who calls on you consistently to render some aid. It is not easy for me to say no to anyone. My belief is if I refuse to help a friend or neighbor, how can I expect I will be taken care of by friends and neighbors when I get to be a little old lady in need? (Of course, I never plan to be a little old lady in need!) I also understand why some people don't step up to help a neighbor. They don't want to get involved with that person's drama and neediness. It is safer to just stay out of it completely.

When I was taking care of my grandmother after my father died, she would ask me why would I spend so much time with her. I replied with the belief I just mentioned: if I ignored her, how could I expect my grandkids to help take care of me if and when I ever need it?

You certainly can be helpful, but you don't need to let anyone consume your life. You don't need to answer the phone at 3:00 in the morning, you don't need to drop everything you are doing to go do everything that other person needs done—that seemingly must be done right now.

One morning, my son called me and mentioned he had

to call Social Security to see how to sign his daughter up to get it, and his refrigerator died and he needed to find someone who could come haul it off. Since he was working, I said I would take care of those things for him. After I hung up, I realized I didn't have time to do it either! I texted him and said I had just agreed to do something I didn't have time to do, so I was stepping back out of it. He laughed and did it himself. (We recently had been talking about how I was doing unnecessary things for other people that were taking up a lot of my time.)

You help a lot of people. Let someone help you! My friend Roxy told me I have helped people so much I have "overpaid my account!" Perfect! (And right after that, I got a statement from one of my credit card companies showing I had overpaid my account by $499!)

Here is another place where you can set some boundaries: when you are invited to attend events and get-togethers. I like to go to workshops, lectures, meditation sessions, parties, memorial services, potlucks, conferences and meetings. But sometimes, I just don't want to go. I now say I have other plans, which is *true*. I always have plans of things I want to do when I have a few free hours. I have been getting messages lately that I need to rest and just sit in the quiet. A lot of messages are telling me that! Guess I had better start listening. I have to sit down and receive my next inspiration and direction. So, I must set boundaries with how I invest my time.

～✧～

BOTTOM LINE: If you keep helping people, you are interfering with their life path. Get out of the way and let them have their own experiences.

ABUNDANCE COMES TO ME FROM EVERY DIRECTION

Money represents spiritual energy.
That's why we call it "currency."

~~∞⊙⊙∞~~

I have been fortunate to have chosen a family that was upper middle class with never any financial struggles. Even when Ed and I got married, we started out with enough money to buy our furniture and get ourselves set up. We were always able to get everything we needed, whenever we needed it.

Marianne Williamson, famous author and lecturer, once told the story of how she had lost $10,000 in an investment that went bad. She felt like a failure and was embarrassed to tell her father what happened. His reaction? He told her how proud of her he was that she was able to absorb the loss!

On a smaller scale, about 15 years ago, one of our tenants paid the rent half in cash and half in a check. I laid the money on the seat next to me and drove to our office. It was a really windy day, and the money must have blown out of the car when I got out. I didn't realize it until later when there was nothing I could do about it. I just made the day for the person who found three one hundred dollar bills blowing by in the wind. That person could have just prayed for some financial relief, and it showed up miraculously. He is probably still telling that story!

What are your thoughts when you have to pay more than $3.00/gallon for gas? How about thinking how grateful you are you can afford to fill up your car and that gas is even available?

One year, our rental properties were hemorrhaging money with all the repairs they needed: a roof, a water heater, a paint job, plumbing work. Ed lost his wedding ring, so we had to get a replacement, *and* our car needed some expensive repairs, all at the same time. I was getting overwhelmed with the money flowing out of our life. I asked my Guides what was going on, and they reminded me that money always flows in and then flows out. In some years, a lot of money flowed in from our real estate business. They said this particular year was allowing us to support the economy. We supported the roofer, the plumber, the jeweler, the painter and the mechanic. We were fortunate enough to be able to do that. And after all that, we were still just fine financially. We are always taken care of.

Can you even imagine having all your bills paid off? We paid off our house one time (for a very short time!), and it was so bizarre to remember to pay the taxes and insurance manually, not as part of a mortgage payment. We are just so used to paying off debt.

Tap into the frequency of abundance. When you play in that frequency, you will have so much fun watching money come to you from every direction. But abundance does not only mean money. Winning a gift basket or free tickets to a concert are also forms of abundance. We can have whatever we want—we just don't realize it.

<hr>

BOTTOM LINE:
Go out and buy something that makes you feel rich.

DID YOU EVEN KNOW YOU HAD ONE OF THOSE?

Pass that stuff on to someone who can use it.

We all have so much *stuff!* Why do we think we need to hang on to all of it? We fill our houses and garages and let it spill over into storage rooms.

What is it that makes it so hard to let go of something we have had since we were kids? I have recently gone through every drawer and closet in my house and gotten rid of a ton of stuff. I was quite proud of myself. I gave away all of it because it was too much trouble to try to sell it. If you came into my house and said you liked something, it was yours.

I have a dresser in a guest room with nothing in it! That gives me a place to put a bunch more treasures I absolutely need. I have empty shelves in bedroom closets and empty cupboards in the garage. It feels clear and freeing to have all this open space. When you move stuff out of your house, you change the energy of the whole place. Start the project by doing just one room a day. Don't try to do the whole job in one weekend. I have fun "shopping in my closet," and I find blouses or shoes I forgot I had! You will probably find you already have everything you need.

When I cleaned out our closet, there was a rifle-cleaning kit, right there on the top layer of our life—and we don't even have a rifle! We gave away close to 500 books to an art school, a woodworking club, a woodturning club, and local libraries. I used to have boxes and boxes of books in the garage, and now, every book I have is on display on one of my bookcases. I can actually find a specific one when I want to lend it to a friend.

Moving is a great way to clear out the closets. Pack up everything and just don't move anything into the new house you don't need or love. Go through all those papers on your kitchen table or desk. Go through the items on your to-do list and DO them. Clear your plate so you can have time to be quiet, meditate, write, and think (not plan!)

BOTTOM LINE:
Clearing out the junk in your house changes the energy and makes room for something new to come in. (Just be careful that the something new is what you *want* to let in!)

JUST SIT DOWN, SHUT UP, AND LISTEN

Keeping yourself busy is an excuse
to keep you from moving forward.

Allow your mind to be still for a minute and pay attention to all the sounds around you. As I wrote this, I was sitting outside in my backyard and started to *listen*. The wind was rustling through the palm trees next to me; a dog was barking (luckily it was far enough away to not be annoying); a car zoomed past my house (I wondered why the driver was in such a hurry); an airplane flew over (think of how many souls with all their "stories" were contained in that small dot); a dove was cooing nearby; kids were playing in their yard. The wind blew the edges of my paper up and down, and it kept hitting the side of my pen.

A mocking bird landed on the back fence and, for the first time in my entire life, I was able to see him (her?) simply open his beak and allow his delightful melodies to pour out. Singing birds sound so playful and full of joy. How can you feel down when all that is surrounding you?

It was a glorious day to sit out there, feeling the cool breeze, sitting in the shade, listening to the bird's song and the children's laughter and giggles. What a joy. What was that day trying to tell me? Every sound I heard had a message for me.

Sirens popped up. Think about it. You never hear sirens unless someone is in serious trouble. Thank heavens the EMTs are on call 24/7 to rush out to help in any way they can. That must be quite a traumatic job. When I volunteered with the Red Cross disaster team, I remember talking with a fireman who had just helped put out a fire in someone's home. He told me he was going to change careers because he was tired of meeting people on the worst day of their lives.

I have been told over and over again by my Guides that I need to sit down and shut up so they can download the information I need to be able to fulfill my mission. My mind is always going a hundred miles an hour, planning, thinking, planning, deciding, organizing, planning, brainstorming, planning. I wear myself out! And then I say I am frustrated because I need to know what my next step is. I keep myself so busy with little stuff, my Guides can't even get through to me. They have all kinds of great ideas for me and are waiting patiently for me to connect with them. When am I ready to tune in?

It is essential for you to step back, rest and relax. Learn to let go of your to-do items just for 10 minutes. As you relax, have a notepad and pen handy. Every time a need-to-do pops up, write it down and get it out of your mind. Put it on the shelf and if you need to do it, you will be reminded to pick it up again. Tune your mind from one station to the next until you find the one that is broadcasting information for *you*.

BOTTOM LINE:
Visualize yourself floating on the top of a pond.
Make yourself so still your body doesn't
even send out any ripples through the water.
Can you possibly be that still?

HANGOVERS ARE NO FUN!

When are you ready to stop doing that?

❦

My mother was a diligent non-drinker. Dad would have a martini or two before dinner quite often, but Mom decided years ago to stop drinking because she saw how many people made complete fools of themselves when they got drunk.

When I was in my senior year at Arizona State University, Ed was serving a year in Vietnam. I was a member of Chi Omega sorority, so I lived in the Chi O dormitory. I had a group of friends who would go over to "The Sands," a bar in a local hotel near the campus. We would be there for sure every Friday for Happy Hour. I was quite proficient in out-chugging most of the guys in the group. Usually I was back at the dorm, passed out by 7:00, while all my sorority sisters were getting ready for their dates. One of the seniors actually wanted to sit me down to do an intervention!! I just heard about that recently from one of my friends. I thought that was so funny, since I knew exactly what I was doing all the time and was in complete (almost) control. It just felt good to have a few beers to relax and go to bed early.

After we got married, the only time we would have a drink or two would be at parties—never just sitting around the house. About once a year, I would really overdo it and end up standing in someone's living room sobbing about something. I made Ed agree that if I ever did that again, he needed to get me the heck out of there!

Eventually, we had our two boys, and that was a game-changer. I can remember those hangovers where we would

28

try all the latest remedies to keep it from happening or to lessen the results if it did. I finally gave it all up when the kids would always get up at about 6 am, with no concern at all that their mother would rather die than get out of bed. I guess I finally grew up and got responsible. It just was not worth it to me any more to have a little bit of fun at night that would be followed by a *lot* of misery in the morning.

This is another example of how our Guides arrange things to happen so we will make the necessary shifts in our lives. We have a bigger mission now that requires us to be in our best shape. I had the experience of drinking and don't need it anymore. I still have a drink maybe every month or two, but I never have more than one. It doesn't feel good anymore.

BOTTOM LINE:
Many times, the decisions that shape your life
get made for you. You just have to pay
attention and recognize it.

GOD DON'T MAKE
NO JUNK

*Maybe how you look is exactly the way
you are supposed to look.*

When you look in the mirror, what do you say to your-self? Do you ever notice what looks pretty good rather than what is wrong? Can you ever be satisfied with how much you weigh? What if how much you weigh is exactly the perfect weight for you? What if you are a little pudgy? What if that is the perfect *you?*

When you see people who keep getting plastic surgery to tweak how they look, do you wonder if they simply can't accept how they were created in the first place? Do they think they can improve on the original model?

Whether you believe it or not, you are the Light of the World—*your* world. Everyone is living in his or her indi-vidual world, and everyone else shows up in that world for the benefit of that person. I showed up in your world for you, and you showed up in mine for me. Each one of us has the power to form our own life experience. Don't negate how powerful you are. Look at your life as it is today. You have co-created every bit of it. Every single thing that hap-pens "to" you is on purpose to move you in the direction that has gotten you to where you are today. Pay attention to how you are being guided into different experiences that are molding you into the exquisite human being you are. Your life is exactly the way it is supposed to be, or it would shift to another path. You cannot make a mistake. When we mess up, we can finally learn and move past the need to repeat the experience over and over.

I have always had a problem with the saying that you need to love yourself. Finally, I heard a statement that I could relate to: *Accept yourself.* When you stop trying to change how you are, you will find so much peace of mind. It is much easier to just *accept* yourself with all your flaws and imperfections than to try to *love* yourself when behind the scenes you feel so messed up.

BOTTOM LINE:
Keep reminding yourself
of *Who You Really Are.*

IS THE RED CROSS ATTRACTING DISASTERS?

You bring in what you focus on.

I spent 4 years volunteering at the local Red Cross office, and as usual, I fully immersed myself in it, working in 4 different areas that interested me. One was being a team leader for the Disaster Action Team on my side of town. I would be on call for a week at a time, once or twice a month, to respond to any local disaster caused by fire, storms, flooding, explosions, etc. I enjoyed doing this, but sometimes, I had other plans and did not want to get a call to respond, especially when the grandkids came over and we wanted to go to a movie.

I would set my intention that the pager would not go off until after they went home. Now, why is it OK for your house to burn down only when it is convenient for me to respond? I began to think about it and realized that all the people at the Red Cross are focused *constantly* on disasters, and guess what? Disasters happen all the time. I decided maybe I should withdraw my focus and perhaps fewer disasters would show up. I asked my guidance about it and the message I got was I did not need to withdraw just yet since the Red Cross needed my organizational mind and since I did not get emotionally distraught after every fire. I didn't "take it home with me." I was guided to stay for a couple more years and then an entirely new path showed up for me—the Arizona Enlightenment Center. I was not able to stay involved with disaster relief as well as with manifesting the vision for the Center that was showing up in a big way.

I know I was valuable to the Red Cross since I did not have a "real job", and I did not have small children to take care of. I was available pretty much at any time. I remember hearing the head of our local chapter say one time, "We don't ask for much—just your time, your money and your blood!" It really is an exhausting experience, especially when you volunteer to go out of town to one of the major disaster responses, such as 9/11, huge floods, fires, or hurricanes. Then you agree to go for three weeks with a moment's notice.

It was a life-changing experience while I was involved, but I knew when I first signed up that it was my *next* step, not my *final* step. I did that until it was time to do something else

If you want to know what you are attracting, look around at who and what is in your life. You have brought all of that in with your power to co-create the circumstances that surround you. You are the one who has come up with the precise mix of ingredients to bake the masterpiece of your life.

BOTTOM LINE:
If you don't like your results, tweak the recipe.
Change the ingredients and bake it again.

GO AHEAD, HAVE THAT MELTDOWN

You cannot do everything by yourself.

When Ed's Parkinson's symptoms started to progress, it was taking a lot of my energy to take care of everything. As the disease got worse, he was no longer able to do *anything* around the house that I was so used to having him do.

I have always prided myself in being independent, so I proceeded to take over the responsibilities for everything in and around the house as well as all the financial details (which I had been doing anyway since we got married). I did it all—because I could. In 2014, our 24-year-old grandson Anthony moved in with us. The moment he got here, I felt like safety had moved in because he is pretty tough and could handle any kind of threat that might pop up (even though I don't spend a lot of time in fear of anything bad ever happening to us). He also could do all the heavy work that needed to be done. I was so relieved and didn't even realize how much I needed some help.

That summer, our water heater went out, and I had scheduled it to be replaced on a Wednesday morning. It is located in a very bizarre little closet in the kitchen next to the washer and dryer and is quite difficult to replace. I had an estimate from one company of $750, but I had called the company that had replaced our neighbor's water heater and knew this company would know how to deal with this bizarre closet. Well, that morning, as I was heading off to our weekly Metaphysical Studies Group, I got a call from the plumbing company that was coming to replace the unit, and the caller told me it would be $1200!!!

I immediately called off the installation, telling him that I had a previous quote for $750. I had been so busy that week, we had already gone three days without hot water because I didn't have time to even make the call. This meant we would not have hot water for a couple more days. (This was not really a big deal, though, because it was July in Phoenix!)

All this finally got to me, and I had a major melt down. I was *so* tired. With tears running down my cheeks, I headed to the meeting, making a gallant effort to get myself under control by the time I got to the group. Unfortunately, I had no luck. I just kept on crying. I *had* to attend the meeting because I was bringing the projector the speaker needed for her presentation. Otherwise, I would have aborted the mission. Then I realized I was going to a meeting filled with my spiritual family, and what better place to be than with them when I was going through all that? I had never met this speaker, and I greeted her with red eyes and runny nose and tears still flowing. By the way, her topic was "What is Happiness and How Can I Get Some?" Ha! I continued to cry through most of the meeting, and I just told everyone I was having a meltdown and knew they would understand. I had not realized how much I needed some help and relief from having to do everything myself.

BOTTOM LINE:
Be willing to admit you need some help.
And be willing to accept it when it is offered!

EVERYONE IS A MANIPULATOR— EVEN YOU!

We just want to create favorable conditions for ourselves.

Everyone is a manipulator. Sounds pretty harsh, but it is true. When we want people to do something for us or with us, all of us present our case in a way that will convince them to support us. We could win the Salesman of the Year award for our efforts in maneuvering people to join us. We unconsciously plan our words carefully before we talk to someone so we can talk him over to our side. We have been doing it since we were little kids. We fine-tune our sales presentations to get what we want.

And is that a bad thing? Absolutely not! We are simply arranging the circumstances of our lives to our liking. We are very powerful. Every one of us.

There really are no *evil people*, just *fearful people* acting in evil ways. Many people have endured extremely painful lives, and they develop the ability to protect themselves and to make themselves feel safe. They learn that nobody else is going to do it for them, so they have to figure out how to take care of themselves. And that is how they learn to manipulate others to get what they want and need.

Be proud of your kids when you see them "working you" to get what they want. They are learning to be Master Manipulators. (I guess it sounds better to say "Master Manifestors.")

When we need a decision from our Mom and Dad or the couple across the street, we know which one we can talk to in order to get the result we want.

When we select an outfit to wear, in addition to making us feel good, we do it to please the eye of our friends. When we look good, others react to it and compliment us on our appearance. We made them feel better when they looked at us. (We "manipulated" them into feeling better.)

Ed was so wise and gentle. If he wanted me to change a behavior (for example, to load the glasses into the dishwasher from the back to the front of the top rack), he would say, "Hey, I need your help." A clever, innovative manipulator.

We invest an enormous amount of time manipulating the behavior of other people. You don't realize how much time you spend paying attention to what others are doing and getting them to do things your way. That keeps you out of living your own life, and it does not allow the other people to have their own experiences.

BOTTOM LINE:
People do what they think they need to do to make themselves feel safe, protected, and in control.

YOU REALLY *ARE* GETTING MESSAGES

*Your Guides are communicating
with you all the time.*

I had always wanted to go to Hawaii and swim with the dolphins, and when I found out Doreen Virtue had scheduled an event to do just that, I declared to Ed I was going. He looked at the flyer and decided he wanted to come along. He had never been to anything like that, and I was not sure I wanted any skeptical energy going with me. I didn't know how he would handle some of the exercises I knew we would be doing. Just before we were to leave, he started having second thoughts about spending that much money on one week in Hawaii ($4000 each!). I got a little smart aleck and announced I was going for sure and he needed to decide if he was going to come along with me.

Just after that, our CPA called to say we were going to get a "boatload" of money back from our taxes since we had overpaid our estimates: approximately $7350!! That removed any doubt about whether both of us were going. It is also an example of what it is like to get a message you are supposed to do a specific thing.

We started the week out with an exercise where we were supposed to walk around the grounds of the hotel and go up to something and ask, "Are you my teacher?" If we got a "yes" signal, we were to ask for a message. Ed walked up to three little birds and asked if they were his teacher and got a firm "no" when they all flew away. Then he walked up to a garden full of Bird of Paradise flowers waving back and forth in the wind. He asked one of them if it was his teacher, and it started to shimmy very quickly. He took that as a "yes" and asked for a message. He heard in his mind that he was doing exactly what he was supposed to be doing and when "they" needed him to do something else, they would let him know.

A couple days later, we did that same exercise one more time, and once again, Ed asked if there was something else he needed to know. He then heard in his mind an answering machine saying, "You have no new messages!" This was happening with someone who had never gotten a message about anything before (or at least someone who did not realize he probably had been getting messages from his Guides for years and never recognized it).

When a thought pops into your mind indicating you should do something or go somewhere you had not considered before, your job is to recognize that and *follow* the guidance. There is a reason you got that thought. You are about to meet someone or experience something new to shift your life in a new direction.

BOTTOM LINE:
Pay attention. Be willing to listen and
follow what your Guides tell you.

ALL THESE REGRETS KEEP POPPING UP!

Nobody holds your mistakes
against you more than you do.

It is so easy to keep beating ourselves up when we mess up—again. You would think we would finally get it and never do it again, but no-o-o-o-o! We keep falling into the same deep hole.

But what if every time you fall into that same hole, you learn a new way out? What if you don't get as beat up as last time? What if you can share your experiences with someone else so that person can avoid falling into that same hole?

You have probably said at least one or two things in your lifetime that you regret. For some reason, all the stupid, inconsiderate things I have said or done have been popping up in my mind lately. I still feel really bad about what happened—but I can never feel bad enough to make it go away. So how is it serving me now to feel bad about something I can't change? I would be willing to bet that at least 80% of the people I hurt with my words or deeds don't even remember *me*, let alone what I said or did!

If you find yourself rehearsing over and over some things you did that were not exactly coming from your loving self, practice rehearsing all the things you have done that were very helpful, kind and considerate. I am pretty sure you will recognize that you have a higher percentage of good things in your past than bad ones. Focus on those. Get some paper and write down all the stupid things you regret. Then list 5 wise things you have done for each stupid thing. Go back and rewrite the end of the story. And go back and burn the pages listing the stupid things. Read the good list every day. That is who you really are.

These regrets that keep popping up, hoping to remind you of how awful you are, come as a gift from your ego, trying to talk you out of being willing to step into your highest potential. Thank it for sharing and send it out to play so you can move forward.

The word "sin" is actually a term from archery meaning "to miss the mark." So, if you have "sinned," you have simply missed the mark. The usual interpretation in organized religion is that if you have "sinned," you have done something that needs to be punished. Yet, you have simply made a mistake, and that can always be forgiven and corrected.

One of the main teachings I have gotten from my study of *A Course in Miracles* is when I feel upset about something to remember to ask for another way to look at it. Your new perspective will pop in either instantly or in a day or two. Suddenly, you have a new understanding of why you or someone else did that thing that left you feeling regret. You can move back into peace.

∽∾⊙⊙∣⊙⊙∾∽

BOTTOM LINE: We don't come with Owner's Manuals. If you could have done better, you would have.

FISHES AND LOAVES

There is always enough.

When Ed passed, we had the service in the same room where we have our weekly Metaphysical Studies group. At first, I made the comment to the group that it would be very casual, and we would not even have any food or drink set up. The group was not in alignment with that, so I said, "OK, just let Judy know what you want to bring so she can organize it." At the end of the meeting, only two people told her they planned to bring something, so I gave her some money to buy some cookies and something to drink. It is not easy to plan when you have no idea how many people would attend and who would bring something to eat.

That morning, people kept coming in and filling the room, so we had to pull in chairs from every nook and cranny in the church. *And,* people kept bringing in plates and plates of food to share with the group. Enough came in to be able to feed the entire crowd of 150 people. After the service, as I was driving home to spend more time with the family, I realized I would need to offer food to all of them. I had it handled for the dinner the night before, but I never even thought about lunch the next day! Well, we had another "fishes and loaves" moment, because we were able to put out what we had on hand, and it was enough for the whole afternoon—and we even had leftovers!

We have a group meeting on Wednesdays where usually 45-55 people come every week. Our "chair committee" does not know how many chairs to set up, but it is amazing to watch. Every time I think they have set up too many, people keep coming in until almost all the chairs are filled. They seem always to intuitively have enough chairs set up. It is a "reverse fishes and loaves" event. We have the chairs available for each person who decides to come that day. There is always a place for everyone!

BOTTOM LINE:
All of us are completely taken
care of in *this* moment.

CONSCIOUS FOOD, CONSCIOUS EATING, CONSCIOUS SOCIETY

Do you really need that Buster Bar?

~•~

If we lived in a truly conscious community, no one would even make soft drinks, cupcakes, candy bars, cigarettes, alcohol or donuts! Walk into one of those convenience stores attached to gas stations and look at the products available for sale. Probably 95% of everything for sale that is edible is not what you would consider a healthy food choice. (They do offer bananas and apples, though!)

I have a dream of living in a community where everything you can buy to eat contributes to the health of your body—organic, pure, very little refined sugar, pesticide free. Can you even imagine what you would feel like if you only consume food that supports the health of your body? Kids would not even have the choice to pick up a cookie or candy bar (unless it was made consciously with healthy, organic ingredients). After a few years, the new children will be born into this lifestyle, and they will have no idea what it would be like to eat in a way that could undermine the health of their bodies.

I watched a commercial tonight for some medication that ended with all the disclaimers about everything that could happen to you if you take it. One possible side effect could be death! In a conscious society, who would develop a medication that could possibly kill someone? I know many medications are very effective and help many people, but why approve one that has the chance of killing someone?

I want to have a business that offers nutritious home-cooked meals that can be delivered to your door every day so you don't have to spend any time trying to think up what to have for dinner. Every menu item will be prepared with love and the best ingredients available. It is completely possible to prepare healthy desserts and snacks to go with the entrees and salads. I actually have a domain name reserved at GoDaddy called "Conscious Catering—For You, For Your Family, For Your Friends." It is filed away for the future when the time is right.

Years ago, my granddaughter and I were playing around with the idea of a cookbook filled with healthy recipes called "Don't Tell the Kids." Our first recipe was for chocolate pudding that is made with bananas and avocado! We didn't want the kids to know there was avocado in it. There are all kinds of recipes you can use to sneak in healthy ingredients and your picky kids would have no idea—well, maybe not the picky kid, but you could probably get passed the kids who are willing to try something new!

Give this recipe a try and see if you like it:

Put one banana, one small avocado, 1 T organic raw honey, 1 heaping T cocoa (or cacao), and 1/4 cup almond milk (or regular milk or water) into a blender and blend till smooth. You can add a little more sweetener to taste and a little more liquid if it is too thick. It's good at room temperature or chilled it in the fridge for a couple hours. It is great plain or with some nuts, over bananas and strawberries or over pound cake.

BOTTOM LINE: Vote with your dollars to support companies that offer products that contribute to your health.

HATEFUL GLARE FROM A BOSTON FAN

I just smiled at her as she sat down.

The Phoenix Suns have really been struggling to pull everything together lately with lots of new players and coaches. They can hardly ever win a game. However, they have a *lot* of really talented young players who could dominate their conference if they can ever get on the same page. We do understand that it will take a few years to develop them—a lot of them are still teenagers!

We have had season tickets for 15 years. This year, every game feels like a home game for the visiting team! The Suns fans are dwindling, so there are plenty of seats for Lakers fans, Toronto fans, Golden State fans, and on and on. I recently attended a game when we were playing the Boston Celtics. There were a *lot* of Celtics fans in the arena. For some reason, the Suns had a strong start and hardly missed a scoring opportunity while the Celtics couldn't buy a basket. We were up by 20 points throughout most of the game. I had Celtics fans sitting in the row in front of me and in back of me. When we were doing so well, my smug thought was, "We have really shut those guys up!" It felt good to be winning for a change. Usually, since the team loses most of the games, we are just grateful for a good play!

Well, we still led into past the middle of the fourth quarter, and then the Suns started missing every shot and the Celtics hit every one of theirs. We lost the 20-point lead and ended up going into overtime when the Celtics won.

By then, their fans were really loud and obnoxious. The woman in front of me stood up (she was in the *front* row upstairs) and blocked my view of the entire court. I was leaning to the right or left to try to see around her. Finally, her husband (who was sitting down) noticed and tapped on her arm to let her know I could not see. She proceeded to turn around and give me a hateful *death stare.*

I felt that stare for about two days after the game and spent a lot of time processing it. It pointed out to me that sports can be one more thing that divides us, along with religion, politics, borders, languages and school pride. That lady is probably a very nice person, and I know that I am a very nice person. Why would we let something like a game stir up so much resentment? *Then,* I realized I had done the same thing to the Celtics fans when we were winning—being so proud we had shut them up with our great play. So many times, we don't realize that when we are upset with someone's behavior, we often have behaved the same way!

BOTTOM LINE:
I could have stood up.

LITTLE JEWELS

A message from my pizza box:
Enjoy Your Delicious Moments.

Ed used to say life happens to us in "little jewels." Those are the times when something special or inspiring happens to bless our day. It happens when someone invites several people over for dinner, and it is a perfect blend of personalities. The evening is relaxing and fun, and the food is fabulous. If you pay attention, you will be able to recognize little jewels throughout your life experiences.

In 2005, Ed and I were on a long ten-week RV trip to visit friends and family all over the country. One afternoon in Colorado, we came up over a hill and saw a herd of buffalo on one side of the road. We got out of the RV, walked up to the fence and for about thirty minutes, we watched this tranquil scene. As we stood there, we watched the babies staying close to their mothers, and we could actually hear the buffalo chewing the grass. A little jewel! (*And*, believe it or not, on the other side of the road from the buffalo roaming, there were antelopes playing!)

Last summer, I went with my friend Cindy up to Flagstaff just for a little adventure and to get out of the record heat we were having in Phoenix. I saw the projected high for the day was to be only 85°, so that's where we headed.

We lucked out with the traffic and had no delays coming or going. We planned to take a ride up the scenic chairlift at the Snow Bowl ski resort just outside Flagstaff. Before we drove up the hill, we decided we should pop by somewhere and pick up a sweatshirt since it could be cold at the top of the mountain. We rejected going to Ross or Target and settled on Goodwill where they sell clothes by the pound. Cindy got one for 62¢ and mine was an upper-class version for $1.07!!

We had to wait until 1:00 to get on the chairlift because of a thunderstorm in the area. Once again, we were lucky we had our jackets and I picked up a couple of plastic ponchos before we got on the ride. After maybe three minutes, it started to rain, and soon we could hear screams from the people in chairs ahead of us as the hail started crashing down! We ended up wrapped in the thin plastic ponchos with rain pouring in through the face opening and running down our sleeves. I swear the water had to be dripping from the chair directly into my shoes. There was absolutely nothing we could do about it—no way to speed up the lift, no way to stop the rain and wind. We felt so sorry for everyone who got stuck on the ride wearing only shorts and T-shirts with no poncho to block some of the rain. The temperature gauge in our van showed a *seventy* degree change from when we left Flagstaff to when we arrived back in Phoenix!

We kept joking about sitting on a wet *metal* chair, going up to the top of a mountain with lightening striking all around us! Eventually we just started singing Jingle Bells at the top of our lungs and making the best of a real mess. But underneath it all, we were not one bit afraid because we are *positive* we have work to do here at this time on the planet and we *knew* we would certainly survive that trip. It will be a trip that we will never forget! A little jewel.

BOTTOM LINE: Remember to be specific
about what kind of adventure you are asking for!

ARE YOU A BULLY?

Why is it fair game to be so rude?

In our current political atmosphere, many of the talk show hosts and TV personalities spend a lot of time making fun of the president—every president—both Bushes, Obama, Trump—members of Congress, other political leaders, Hollywood stars, athletes, etc. As I watch those shows, I wonder if these people realize they are actually bullies. I am sure if someone at school bullied their grandchildren or children, they would be making an appointment with the principal to take action against the bully. Why is it OK for them to be bullies themselves? I imagine they don't even realize it. They think they are very clever with their jokes. This goes on with both political parties. I guess they see it as just a game and a way to entertain their audiences and raise their ratings. We need to stop it. Stop supporting those shows. Stop participating. Are you willing to stop?

Kids can have a hard time getting through school. Bullying is a big topic now in the news. I can remember hearing people say, "That's just the way kids are." Well, it's not the way kids *should* be, and we need to stop allowing it and blowing it off thinking the bullied ones will get over it. The bullies are the ones with the problem. They are wounded and need to do something to knock someone else down if that kid seems to be smarter or smaller or weaker. It helps them feel better to put someone else down. It is not OK. We have to be part of the solution to start the change.

Many teachers have been able to diffuse the tension between a couple of their students by putting them on a project together. As they work on the assignment, they *have* to spend time together, and they might just find out that the other one is not so awful as they connect on a human level.

I love seeing stories about people who used to hate each other making a total shift into forgiveness. It just takes a minute to change the complete atmosphere in a room, in a neighborhood, in a meeting, in an organization. It only takes one person to be willing to step up and offer peace. It takes courage, because there is a chance of being attacked. Just one small step can change everything.

BOTTOM LINE:
Are you willing to be the
first one to forgive?

I HAD AN INNER VOICE GUIDING ME AS A KID

You are not in this alone.

I have had a lot of friends who are intuitive and have been aware of it since they were babies. I have always *wanted* to be intuitive, but I certainly never noticed anything special like that about me as I was growing up. However, now that I am looking back at my life, I realize I had a very mature Inner Voice with me since I was little. The first time I ever heard it was when I was maybe five years old. I was attached at the hip to my older brother. He is two years older than I am and we did *everything* together. One day, while I was taking a nap, he went to a movie with one of his friends. When I woke up, I was devastated…but I heard this very mature voice say, "It is time for Johnie to be able to go somewhere occasionally with a friend, and you can stay home and play on your own. He still totally loves you as his little sister, and that will never change. You don't need to think you are losing him." As I look back at that day, I can still hear that voice, and I can remember agreeing that he really did need to be able to go somewhere without me.

I do remember, though, my mother seemed to have a bit of "lack consciousness" because she often talked about how we might not have enough money to pay some of the bills. I was in junior high school at the time, and I felt safe enough that I decided I would not start to worry about money until my parents started selling off some of our furniture and other belongings—and that never happened. My Inner

Voice kept reminding me we were just fine, and we always had everything we needed. However, I also remember how bad I felt every time I lost or broke my glasses. Besides knowing that it would be several weeks before I would be able to see clearly again, my first thought was always how bad I felt to have to tell Mom and Dad they would have to pay for new glasses for me one more time!

BOTTOM LINE:
We are never alone and left to twist
in the wind all by ourselves.

QUIT MAKING STUFF UP

*Most of the time, we have no idea
what is really going on.*

I realized I had been holding on to Ed because I thought I might be afraid to be home by myself at night. I was making up all kinds of scenarios about what could happen when I would be in the house alone.

I need to stop trying to figure anything out. Stay out of the future and stop making up stories about what "might" happen. *Right now,* I am OK. I can learn to become the observer and rise above the battlefield and just watch what is going on. Do I really think my Guides would allow anything to hurt me or scare me in the middle of tonight? I am so protected. *Nothing* will be able to harm me. I am stronger than any darkness that tries to overcome or connect with me.

Sometimes we make up stuff to protect ourselves. I didn't like my "cavalier attitude" about Ed's situation, feeling like I was being insensitive about what was happening with him, like it was no big deal. I pretended it was not as bad as it really was. But I see now it was a form of denial, because the alternative was that I would spend my life crying and in depression and fear. So, I shut that out and made up a story that I could easily handle it all.

Whenever I don't see some of my friends for a few weeks, I make up stories about what is going on with them. Not anything dramatic—I am just coming up with all kinds of things that could be happening to them. And then it would be crazy to hear what had really been going on that had nothing to do with anything I had imagined.

Notice what we do when we see something we have never seen before. We immediately cycle through the files in our brain to explain what it is. If we can't find anything, we start making stuff up. We compare that thing to something we have seen sometime during our life. If that is not an airplane, what is it? We decide it is a UFO! And it actually is a UFO—an Unidentified Flying Object. That doesn't necessarily mean it is from outer space! It is just unidentified to us at that moment.

I woke up in a funk recently and was focused on what was going wrong in everyone else's life. Almost everyone I know is in a huge trauma drama. I could write it all out, but I don't want to give it any energy. Again, do I *really* know what is going on in their lives? I am making stuff up again.

Am I going to practice what I preach and focus on the stuff that is working? This is a test. I know I am here to hold the light for others who are off balance. They all need to go through their own experiences so they can shift into a new consciousness. I don't know their true story, but they do, and their Guides can help them through it.

BOTTOM LINE:
The third agreement in the book, *The Four Agreements* by Don Miguel Ruiz, is "don't make assumptions." Learn to ask questions to be sure you understand what is really going on with someone.

BE WILLING TO DO SOMETHING DIFFERENT

It's time to let go of the past.

We are such creatures of habit. We feel safe doing the same things over and over. We go into a restaurant and order the same entrée we have always ordered. No way would we order something we have never tried. We know we love the usual meal, and we don't want to take a chance of messing up the evening by ordering something we might not like.

Can you be daring enough to try something new? Can you possibly not sit in the same seat at a weekly meeting? Are you allowed to sit on the other side of the room? Can you sit in a different pew at church? Remember how families seemed to have certain pews reserved every Sunday? This is the Clarke family's pew. That is the Anderson family's pew. Heaven forbid a new family would come in and sit there! How would we handle that?

Brush your teeth with you left hand (unless you are already left-handed!). Move your furniture around in your house. Hang the pictures in a different place. Stop weighing yourself every morning. Put the scales away!

I did something daring this year and did not renew my season tickets for the Phoenix Suns. We have had them for 15 years, and I was willing to step outside the circle and let go of them. (BUT my son Dan and his wife did renew, so it does not really count as a great sacrifice.)

Get up in the morning and allow things to happen. Be

flexible. Be spontaneous. Be willing to change your plans. One night last summer, my granddaughter and I were talking and realized we both had four days when neither of us had anything on our schedules. At 7 pm we decided to go to San Diego, and we left at 8:30. I love to be spontaneous!

We have in-ground trash cans in our neighborhood, but many neighbors are using the new big containers that can be rolled out to the sidewalk. I finally got one of those and used it for the first time since 1973. It feels pretty good. Much easier. This is symbolic of my being willing to let go of the past.

When you try something different, get your journal and write some thoughts about how you feel, how you have changed. If it feels good, keep looking for new ways to do something different.

<hr>

BOTTOM LINE:
Throw away the template and try something new.

KILL 'EM WITH KINDNESS

What is the most loving thing
you can do right now?

Wow! I saw a news article recently that was profound. A young woman went into a coffee shop in Tennessee wearing a T-shirt showing support for one side of the current political spectrum in the country. She was harassed for some reason by a few people working in the store. She left and came back later with fifty fellow supporters. They came in peacefully and with a friendly attitude, and the day ended up with everyone ordering coffee and joking together—actually, both sides becoming friends despite their different political points of view. What a beautiful lesson in how to heal the world! I hope to be part of such a demonstration myself someday. (Have you already decided which side was the harassing side and which side was the friendly side?)

I have had a great time in my past trying to win over some clerk or neighbor or fellow shopper who seemed to refuse to smile. I would smile or say a little pleasantry until (usually) I could get a smile back. When I was a teacher's aide in Texas, I liked to focus on the tough kid who always got in trouble to see if I could get him to smile. I knew he had a difficult childhood already and could use a little moment of peace. (And that kind of kid never missed a day of school! His mom needed the break!)

One time, a woman of another race said loudly, "You're welcome!" when she had held the door open for me at the bank, and I didn't make any acknowledgment. I, of course, was oblivious to it since I had a lot of other things on my mind. When she said that, I thanked her so much for helping me and apologized that I didn't recognize her kindness. She finally smiled, and we both ended up in a better place for the rest of the day.

When I was in Egypt, I went with a few friends to a little Circle-K-like store next to the hotel to get some bottled water. I stepped outside and sat on a bench waiting for them to get what they needed. A woman walked by, dressed in the full black burka, but her face was not covered. She looked very stern and on a mission to quickly get to where she was going. We looked at each other, and after a few seconds, we both spontaneously broke into a cheerful smile. I can still feel the love in that moment, reminding me we are alike despite what we have learned about how we should hate each other and feel separate.

BOTTOM LINE:
What can *you* do to add to the peace in the world?

QUESTIONING MY GUIDANCE

How do you know what *to believe?*

Recently, I started receiving messages from several different sources that contradicted each other. Since I usually could trust what they were saying, I got confused as to what I should believe. This could have been labeled a "crisis in confidence," and it really bothered me.

When I get in these moments of confusion, I get out my journal and ask what I need to know about this. I was guided to sleep on it and get my answer in the morning. In the morning, what I got was to stop going outside of myself for answers because I already know what to do. And the second thing I got is that both of these sources are correct some of the time and sometimes they miss the mark.

A few days later, I was sitting at Pep Boys waiting for an oil change for my car and started writing in my journal, asking again about this. I was very concerned that I was not being guided correctly and that I might be passing incorrect information on to my friends. As I was writing, my first thought was "yellow cars." (In our family, we have a tradition that seeing a yellow car means "everything will be OK.") Immediately, I got another thought, "No, you don't need anything outside of yourself. Trust that you will not be misled." I proceeded to completely ignore this advice and started watching the traffic go by. I asked if X were true and watched for yellow cars for 10 minutes. Nothing. Then I asked if Y were true and watched for another 10 minutes. Nothing.

However, I did notice that school buses kept going by…a lot of them. *Yellow* school buses. And then I got reminded I often say I will not let doubt come in and take me off the bus when I am focused on a particular vision. So here was my answer: Don't allow doubt to pull me off my path. I am protected and guided, and I will *know* which way to go and what to believe.

This type of experience is an example of an attempt by our ego to plant doubt in us. Pull those weeds out of your mind! Figure out how to do it gently and in a way that fully and permanently removes them. The low energies are making another desperate attempt to block us and our power. It is a test to see if you will fold. Maybe things just might happen in a different way than you have even imagined. Hmm. There are an infinite number of outcomes/realities.

BOTTOM LINE:
Are you willing to let those low energies win?

WHAT IF I AM ATTACKED WHEN I GO PUBLIC?

Not everyone is supposed *to like you.*
It is in the plan.

One of the excuses we use for not stepping out in public to share our wisdom is we are afraid of being verbally attacked. Do I really have any wisdom that can help anyone? Who do I think I am that someone will want to listen to me? Will my weaknesses be exposed to everyone? Will people think I am stupid? Do I really have the guts to get up and speak in front of hundreds of people? Will they think I talk too fast? Will they think I am saying the same thing every other speaker is saying? Will they question me out loud so I need to give a response? What if I can't think of anything to say? What if my outfit looks awkward? What if I don't stand up straight and my stomach pooches out? What if my hair sticks up in a weird place? What if I forget everything?

We might very well be sharing a message that is controversial to someone with a different belief system. That person may feel "obligated" to point out how wrong we are. Do we need to defend our message?

If someone says something to you or about you and you get offended, deep down you believe what he is saying. It rubs a wound you have from the past and triggers all kinds of emotions. If someone says something about you that you think has nothing to do with you, it won't bother you and you will not be offended at all. Someone might tell you that you are always negative and you never have any positive thing to say, yet you know you are always looking for the good in everyone and everything around you. You don't get offended, because you know you are uplifting and people like to be around you. The person who attacked you is the one with the problem. He probably feels negative and down all the time, and he subconsciously wants to pull you down with him.

Your ego does *not* want you to be unbelievably success-ful. It wants you to stay small, so it will try everything it can to get you to doubt yourself and sit down and shut up. If you can remember this, you will be able to stay strong and not let anything pull you off the bus.

Good for you for being willing to step up and give some-thing new a try. Take a chance and be vulnerable. You are so comfortable doing what does *not* challenge you. You are proud of where you are and very happy to stay right there. You can feel your throat tightening. What the heck do you think will happen if you share messages? Sure, you got killed in several lives because of it, but it is finally safe now. You can help someone feel better with what you say. Your words can shift someone to a new level, and you won't even know you did it. Remember, your Guides are speaking through you. You are just an instrument. They have been waiting for you to clear yourself (your instrument) so they can be heard through you.

BOTTOM LINE:
Focus on how to serve and critics won't even notice you.

WHAT YOU ARE SEEKING IS SEEKING YOU

The financial resources and people to help you are available NOW.

If you have a vision developing in your mind, you might feel a little skeptical that you will be able to manifest it. It could be *huge* and way beyond any ability you think you have that could possibly bring it forward.

Remember, if you are given the inspiration, you also are given the way to create it. You will not be led to the edge of the cliff only to be thrown off into the abyss below. You can manifest *anything* you can dream of. *Everything* is possible. You just haven't connected with the resources yet.

Picture yourself as a multi-millionaire. After you have traveled all over to experience every aspect of the world, and after you have set yourself and your family up to be financially independent for life, and after you have given away a good amount to people you know who really need some help, you will one day sit back and say, "What the heck am I going to do now? I am certainly not fulfilled with my current lifestyle, and I need to do something that can help the world." Sit down and brainstorm ideas of how you can help until you can focus on one or two that really inspire you. Don't let yourself get distracted by focusing on everything on your list. Take the time to write out a plan. Get specific with what you want to do. Get a good estimate of how much it will cost. Since you are already a multi-millionaire, you should have the ability to pay cash for your entire project. Doing a project that will be debt-free takes a lot of pressure off your back.

But what if you aren't already a multi-millionaire and you have this inspiration bubbling up inside? If you can spend some time *acting as if* you really are wealthy, you will recognize that when you have way more money than you will ever need, you will be looking around for ways to put it to work to help as many people as possible. That means that if you, the non-millionaire, can connect with someone else, the project-seeking millionaire, together you can do a lot to help change the world. Don't keep sitting around thinking it would be impossible to create your vision. How can you locate and connect with the people who are looking to help in some way?

I have had a hard time most of my life approaching someone to ask for money for any project. But it is easy to do if you present your idea as something that will help the entire neighborhood or community. *You* personally will not benefit from a monetary gift someone may give you. You are asking for the money for a humanitarian project. This has nothing to do with greed. This has to do with helping as many people as you can.

∞⌾∞

BOTTOM LINE:
Focus on pulling the resources to you.
It is time to connect.

WE HAVE A DUTY TO SPREAD THAT RUMOR

I saw it on the internet, so it must be true!

Have you heard the unwritten law that any time you hear a rumor, you are required to spread it to at least ten people? Then you have filled your obligation to keep it alive.

Can you remember when we used to be able to listen to the news, and we would only get the facts of what happened? No opinions. If the station chose, it would occasionally allow its anchor reporter to give an editorial with his personal opinions about a story. It was always clearly labeled as an editorial and not necessarily the view of the station or its advertisers. Most of the time, we would have no idea what the political party was of the broadcasters.

Today, all news is gossip. (Actually, news has *always* been gossip.) Every story is about someone saying something to or about someone else or doing something to someone else. The newscasters' job is to be sure everyone hears what happened that day, and then we get the chance to form an opinion and share it with our family and friends.

Stay vigilant about what you are saying about others. *Never* put comments about someone in a text or email you would not like to be read by that person. Act as if your phone accidentally called the person you are talking about, and you don't know it. If you always speak kindly about everyone, you never have to frantically retrace what you just said. Wanna get away?

But what if you do mess up and say something embarrassing or rude? You don't need to beat yourself up. Every moment is a teaching moment. You will either learn to stop doing it or not. You will keep doing it until you get it, and then you will be done with that type of behavior.

Read the book *The Four Agreements.* The second agreement is to "be impeccable with your word." Don't forget, every time you threw a little dirt, you lose a little ground. People lose a little respect for you every time you gossip about someone. Stay on the high ground.

BOTTOM LINE:
Be the one who stops the further spread of the dirt.

YOU CAN'T DO ANYTHING WRONG

"I am willing to see peace rather than this."
— A Course in Miracles

Think of all the things you have done wrong. Can you accept the idea that you *cannot* do anything wrong? Everything you do teaches you how to do it or how not to do it. If it is a painful experience, you will keep doing it until you don't. Once you understand it is not what you want to do anymore, you will be done with it and never need to do it again. Lesson learned—*finally.*

Many of us carry guilt from something we did years ago. What is the purpose of that guilt? Does it serve you to keep dragging it around with you? You are 50 years old and still holding on to that awful thing you said or did to someone. Why do you think you deserve to keep suffering for that cruel thing you did?

If you remember you can't do anything wrong, it is easier to move past the need to feel guilty. Of course, there *will* be another lesson waiting in the wings, but now you know how to learn it sooner and with ease and grace as opposed to learning with pain and suffering. How you learn is completely your choice. Which way sounds easier? Learn from it, and don't make that same mistake again.

Stop telling your story. Turn the page. Write a new chapter. Stop focusing on what you did "wrong." Don't even talk about it anymore. That only gives the "mistake" energy. And your friends get weary of hearing it over and over. Give it a rest.

Your strong ego may not let you let go. It will keep reminding you of how you screwed up *again*. Be gentle with it as you go around it and move forward. Every experience you have brings a lesson. When you get to the other side, you are a new person, ready to tackle the next lesson with more wisdom and knowledge.

BOTTOM LINE:
Everything that happens to me gives me an opportunity to choose. It's completely up to me. Why would I consciously choose to feel any way other than peaceful?

WHAT THE HECK
AM I DOING HERE?

Stop getting ready to be ready.

We spend a lot of time waiting for something to happen so we can get on with our purpose. It is really a great excuse for not moving forward, isn't it?

Your purpose is _____—for now. It will change as you grow. You are evolving. You don't have to find your ultimate purpose today. Just find what you are being guided toward now. And you don't necessarily have to make a living doing your purpose. Look around at what you have been guided to do in your life. You are being groomed constantly for your life purpose. You may not recognize it because it looks too easy—too comfortable. That's because that *is* what you are supposed to do. It is your purpose—for now. Let someone else have your job if you have lost interest in that position. You have a *new* adventure lining up.

Value the in-between time before you find a new job. You are back in the cocoon. A cocoon is a time-out period—for downloading and transforming. Don't worry about not knowing specifically what you are supposed to do. You have indicated your willingness, and you are now in the process of becoming able to handle the assignment. Be patient. Everything is perfect.

Getting ready to be ready is a diversion. A delay tactic. Sometimes I feel like I am hesitant to really commit to a goal because I am afraid it will actually manifest. It *will* manifest because I am a powerful manifestor and that can be scary.

It is not reasonable to assume I would be given a job to do and not be given all the resources to get it done. I am a messenger who is bringing the idea of the Enlightenment Center to the people who can help manifest it. We are obligated to allow the resources to come through us so we can help change humanity. You can have everything, but you put up blocks because you feel unworthy.

There is never a straight road from where you are to your final destiny. It is like climbing switchbacks up the mountain after being at the bottom of the Grand Canyon. You can see the lodge at the top, but the path takes you over here, then over there, then over here, then over there again—back and forth until you finally get to your destination. The switchbacks (the path) made your life a lot easier than if you had to go straight up the side of the mountain.

Your gifts are meant to be shared, and they were given to you because you are the guardian who has the responsibility to share them in the most effective way. Everyone is waiting for *you*.

***

BOTTOM LINE:
The world needs you to develop your
abilities quickly so you can help heal it.

YOUR GUIDES
ARE ON DUTY

They will let you know if they need your help.

Our son Tim always has loved having a motorcycle. When he first got married and was hardly making enough money to live on, he was happy he "had to have" a cycle since they could not afford a second car. It was like he had no other choice!

He was taking some community college classes, and one night I stopped by their apartment to stay with Anthony, our first grandson, until his wife got home. On the way home, she passed an accident where a motorcyclist had been hit by a car, and it was on the road Tim would have taken to get to class. We both started to panic, wondering if it were Tim. I drove out to the scene and stopped to talk with a policeman who was sitting in his car, writing his report of what happened. I ran up to his car and saw he had the victim's driver's license in his hand, getting ready to contact the family. I was a blubbering maniac as I tried to find out who had been hit and if he was badly hurt. Finally, I looked closely at the license and realized that it was not Tim. Thank God!

I drove as fast I as could back to the apartment to share the good news, and we both sat there crying and feeling so grateful. When he got home, I don't think he had any idea of what nervous wrecks we had been when we thought he was the one who had been hit.

If you ever feel like it is up to you to help someone out of a predicament, step back and remind yourself their Guides do not really need your help. They are totally capable of handling every situation. They will let you know if they need you to step in and do something. You can be their instrument *if* they need you.

My mother grew up in Grove City, Ohio, a small town outside Columbus. She met my father at a drug store soda counter near Ohio State University. Dad joined the Air Force and promptly got stationed in Moultrie, Georgia. They ended up getting married, and Mom soon joined him. She had never been outside the State of Ohio—and there she was in Moultrie, Georgia. Not long after she got there, Dad got sent off on some secret mission he couldn't even tell her about, and she was left there in a strange town, miles from home, all alone. Magically, one day when she was walking downtown, she looked across the street and there was one of her sorority sisters from Ohio State! That little twist of fate completely changed her life, and she was able to survive until Dad got back. Her Guides were very busy setting up that experience for her.

BOTTOM LINE:
Look at your life and see how many times you changed direction. You got to a fork in the road and were guided to shift and go a different way. Wonder how things would have turned out if you had ignore that and kept going in the other direction?

WHAT WAS SHE THINKING WHEN SHE CHOSE THAT OUTFIT?

If you are going to judge,
practice judging in favor.

It is so hard to remember to only say kind things about people. We are critical beings and notice all the things about others we think should be some other way if only *we* were in charge of what they wear and what they do.

When I was in junior high school, my mother made a statement I have remembered to this day: "I have never heard my friend Lorrie say an unkind thing about anyone." What a wonderful thing for someone to say about you!

I recognized many years ago that when you say something negative about someone to someone else, you are actually looking for agreement that what you believe is true. And maybe it could make you feel better about yourself to know everybody else is somehow defective!

However, several times, I have ended up changing my opinion about someone after that person says something negative about someone else. We used to watch a weekly country western music show because everyone on the show seemed to have such a great time. One day, the host, a very sweet guy, made a snide comment about the president, and it affected how I have felt about him ever since.

It is probably not possible for us to not form a judgment about everyone we meet. Give it a try for a day. See if you can get through a full day without first *speaking* a negative comment about someone, and later work on getting through a day without *thinking* anything negative about anyone. I wonder if that is even possible.

When you look at a woman who has a weird hairdo or is wearing a bizarre outfit, don't forget that she likes that hairdo or outfit. She chose it because it made her feel good. She thinks she looks pretty cool. If it is a *really* bizarre outfit, you can look at her with the thought that it took a lot of guts to wear it in public. She has a lot of self-confidence and obviously she does not care what someone else thinks about her. Good for her!

BOTTOM LINE:
Can you look at that crazy outfit or hairdo and say to her,
"I just love how you express yourself"?

SATURDAY MORNING FACEPLANT

How could I fall like that and not break anything?!

This was the first year the Litchfield Park Historical Society organized a Home Tour of some of the magnificent homes in our town. I walked over there with four of my neighbors, and I have to emphasize, we *walked* over there. We put 9000 steps on their FitBits. This is way more exercise than I ever get. I was quite proud of myself for surviving it. As we started back downtown to get some lunch, I guess I was pretty tired and didn't pick up my feet and tripped over a raised crack in the sidewalk. You probably have experienced the slow motion you kick into as you are on your way down. All I could think of was the upcoming broken nose, jaw, and/or teeth I was about to experience.

As I laid there face down, I started to assess the damage and was completely amazed that nothing was broken. All I was dealing with was a huge cut on the inside of my lower lip that was about an inch long and a half inch wide. It was so deep it almost came through my lip.

Interesting how your life can shift in 5 seconds. I had just commented to my friends that it was so nice I had nothing else to do all day but go to the home tour and walk through the art show going on in the park. And the next thing I knew, we were on the way to the ER. Luckily, my neighbor is an MD, so I was in good hands. We called my son Tim, and he and his girlfriend came right over. They had also commented that they had nothing on the schedule for the day, so they were relaxing and going out for breakfast. The call came in before they even ordered.

That night, I put some drops of CBD oil on my lip and swished some liquid silver over the cut. The next morning, that cut had completely closed up…overnight! I know mouths heal quickly, but I don't know if they do it overnight. It didn't heal completely for a month or so, but that hole closed up and never got infected. It never hurt as much as a canker sore can hurt. Miracles!

During the next week, even though my mouth was healing miraculously, my body felt like it had been run over by a truck, and I was *so* tired. I took a bunch of naps—because I could—and that felt good. Then I started analyzing what I could learn from this fall. What was the message?

One friend helped me understand it showed I am always safe and protected. Then I heard a speaker say, "Trust what comes." And then I got that it was a "total system reboot." My outer shell got cracked open so more wisdom can come in. Perfect! I'm ready for my next adventure!

BOTTOM LINE:
When you experience a traumatic event,
it is a signal it is time for a change. It has a message.
What can you learn from it?

WHEN YOU ARE RETIRED, EVERY DAY IS A TUESDAY

*There is nothing else I need
to be doing right now than this.*

Ed and I had been Realtors for over 22 years when we suddenly realized we had enough money saved up so we could retire if we wanted to. It is a strange feeling when you get to where you don't *have* to work anymore. It is a goal most people strive for, yet it is important to have a project, a hobby, a deep interest in some cause to give you a reason to continue to get up in the morning.

We have been retired for quite a few years, yet I still get taken back when someone asks me if I had a good weekend. I have to stop and remember what today is and if the weekend just happened or is about to happen…if it just happened, what the heck did we do? When you are retired, every day feels like a Tuesday or a Saturday. It's funny how you can actually *feel* what day it is. When I wake up in the morning, the first thing that pops in my mind is, "What day is it? What time is it? Am I late? Do I need to get up? What are the plans for the day?" And I *love* it when the answer is I don't need to get up just yet!

Many of my friends are in the middle of changing careers, who they hang out with, what they invest their time in. It is common to not know what the next step is. We are all "mid-leap," ready to land on our two feet and allow our lives to be shifted. This is a most exciting time to be here. If we stop controlling our lives, we have the opportunity to go down completely different paths to a completely different destination. Who knew I would be writing books? Not me! (But then again, I did know I was supposed to write because my Guides kept nagging me for *years* to get started!)

I don't know what happened to all the years in between the beginning of my career and the day I could let go of it. I must say, though, I am so grateful to know what my purpose is. I have been preparing to open the Arizona Enlightenment Center since 2004. I have spent massive amounts of time planning and getting ready for when the time is right. I can see how older people can get depressed when they don't have anything to work on. You can only watch so much TV. The truth is, though, you really do have a reason to be here right now. Everyone who is here now is here on purpose.

❦

BOTTOM LINE:
How are you going to "invest"
your precious time?

YOU ARE AN ALCHEMIST—YOU CAN CHANGE ANYTHING

You can change the world by extending peace.

You have heard of people who are able to change lead into gold, right? That is what alchemy is—the art of "transforming metals." It can also apply to transforming energy.

We have a lot of meetings at our house, so there are many extra cars parked in the neighborhood. Twice in the past couple of weeks, someone parked in front of the house across the street, and the owners had to ask to have the car moved because they were expecting a delivery.

The second time, my friend was coming over to spend some time with me, and she was very concentrated on finding my house. She did not even notice she had partially blocked my neighbor's driveway. When we came out to her car, there was a note on her door very politely asking her to move the car up just a little. My friend felt bad she did that and wrote a kind apology in return, and we put it on the gate to their courtyard.

The next day, I saw the neighbor outside, and I went out to apologize for the parking issues. She was very sweet and said she was so pleased with what a kind note my friend had left. I told her that was because *she* had been so kind in her note and that prompted a kind response from my friend. Look at how peacefully this was handled...no yelling and swearing and declarations of war in the neighborhood. We can all do our part to shift our planet into more harmony just by the way we treat each other. It feels so much better than a fight! And you have an important part in this play.

But what if one day, you didn't handle it so well? What if you got angry and that made the neighbor get angry? You probably don't feel so good about it. No need to beat yourself up—it happened. Now, what are you going to do to shift the energy? Don't be afraid to be the first one to offer an olive branch. *You* are the one. Be the alchemist.

If you are in a meeting or a family gathering that starts to get a little tense, do you want to join in with the arguing that will help build the tension, or do you want to be an alchemist and do what you can to shift the energy in the room? You have the power to say something that can redirect the focus of the conversation, or you possibly can make the shift by just being in the room.

BOTTOM LINE:
You have no idea how powerful you are.

I AM AN INFINITE BEING
AND I CAN HANDLE THIS

Your ego does not want you
to know how powerful you are.

You get placed in the middle of chaos so you can show what it means to be a peacemaker. You are exactly where you are supposed to be. When you are an Infinite Being, you can handle it.

After Tim was born, I went through some tough times with post-partum depression. I was so tired, I thought it would be a relief to just walk in front of a truck and end it all. When he was about 2 months old, I was "guided" to a bookstore and found the book *How to Live 365 Days a Year.* As I read it, I learned I had a choice to be sad or happy, and happy was so much better. Without realizing it, I remembered Who I really was—an Infinite Being—and an Infinite Being would not linger in depression very long at all. I chose to be happy, and I have never been seriously depressed again.

I was unable to sleep through the night for years because Ed was so sick, yet I was able to handle it. You do what you have to do. As an Infinite Being, I was able to stay strong.

Now that Ed is gone, I am here in the house by myself, but that is OK because I am making a breakthrough; it will not be more than I can handle. Just like when I am at the dentist when the Novocain hasn't completely blocked the pain, I can decide to get more and more shots or just suck it up and take a little pain. I can suck it up now, be with the pain and just experience it.

We all used to be healers. That is why when we hurt ourselves, we put our hand on the wound to make it feel better. (We are Infinite Beings!)

You are needed to help heal, and the time is *now*. You have no limitations except what *you* impose on yourself. You are infinite! You can use your ego in positive ways. Bring it with you on your spiritual path. It will give you the guts to do what you need to do.

Don't give up and lose faith. What you are waiting for is right around the corner. Keep priming the pump, the water is just about to start flowing. Things are moving very fast. We are being swept along like a leaf going down a creek. We bump into things on the side, hesitate a little, regroup and move on in a new direction.

Remember, humanity is evolving. All this perceived chaos is like labor pains. We are going through labor, birthing a new humanity. And, oh yeah, you are an Infinite Being! You *can* handle this!

BOTTOM LINE:
"What if you really *are* amazing?" — Debbie Ford

EVERY DAY IS
A GOOD DAY

A "bad day" is just an interesting day.

I can't remember when I last had a bad day. In my opinion, every day is a good day, but when it is not particularly good, it is just an interesting day.

Make your days interesting. Get in the car and get lost and see what you come across. Be flexible moment-by-moment to make a correction in your flight path that just might lead you to the most amazing adventure you have ever had. You have to be willing to be flexible and try something new.

Make the best of your situation. When the Germans kept bombing London, all the buildings were a pile of rubble. The adults were distraught and full of fear, but some of the kids found amazing games to play in those piles of rubble. They were creative enough to make every day a new adventure. They didn't know enough to be afraid.

There is a universal belief that it is not a good thing to be sent to jail or prison. But being in jail is actually just a place to be. It is a perfect place for an inmate to experience everything he signed up for in his Soul Contract. He can think he is a victim, or he can make a difference in someone else's life. It can be the best thing that ever happened to him to make him choose a different path in life.

It is such a drag to be around a guy who complains about everything. He can't even find one good thing that happened all day. He drags everyone around him down into his lower level of vibration. I avoid this kind of person like the plague. It takes a lot of focused effort to stay positive—to find something beautiful to look at or something inspiring to listen to.

It's up to you. How can you soar like an eagle when you are hanging around with vultures? You can be the eagle that brings everyone around you up to a higher frequency. Never be willing to be the one who is dragging everyone else down.

Be the one everyone wants to be around, not the one everyone wants to get away from.

BOTTOM LINE:
What are you bringing to the table?
Are you adding to the love in the world?
Are you making everyone else's day a good day?

YOUR GUIDES ARE TAPPING YOU ON THE SHOULDER

"Your divine purpose was fully funded before you were born." — Courtney Long

I am "supposed" to write 2-3 books yet *this* year! Of course, that sounds daunting—even impossible. But I am learning I don't have to figure out *how* to do something, just be *willing* to do it. Set the intention to do it. Then get out of the way and watch how it comes through. You have no clue, but your Inner Guides know exactly what to do. You just have to have a little willingness to get it done.

If you hate where you work, you are taking up someone else's job. If you are miserable, it is time to move on. Love it or leave it. Don't spend one more day in a job you hate. That hate and unrest are coming in to give you a boot out the door. If you don't have the nerve to quit, your Guides will do it for you.

You have many gifts in this lifetime, and they are not for you to keep under a blanket. You will not be overwhelmed. The only barrier to your service is fear. Deep understanding is in your tissues. Your Guides work with you at night to prepare you. They have work for you to do, and there is no time to waste. You will be placed where you are needed. Work with them to awaken the sleeping ones. Place them into service along with you. Accept this gift, move forward and don't look back. You do not always know what step to take next, but they do.

You are all special—you just need to wake up to it. You are waking up beautifully and are well along on your divine path. You all have your own way of attracting who is supposed to connect with you. You have shown you are willing, so get on with it. Your Guides will help you to access your confidence when you speak with anyone who is brought to you.

Realize you were programmed with your limiting thoughts *long, long* ago, and it is entirely possible to clear them out and replace them with feelings of courage. You have no idea how powerful you are and that you can do *anything*. And don't worry, you will be able to fulfill your purpose without showing off or bragging, "Look at me. I'm special."

As we continue down our path, our guides keep tapping us on our shoulder to help us gather more and more experiences. Every event fine-tunes us just a little more, so by the time we are in the fall or winter of our life, we are finally one of the "wise ones" who can inspire others in their own path. However, we don't really need to wait until we are in the fall or winter. We can decide to catch on to the "system" whenever we choose. We can become one of the wise ones when we are a teenager.

BOTTOM LINE:
Stop resisting what life has planned for you.
Those plans are way better than any you have in mind.

LET'S GET GOING!

Patience itself is my lesson—for now.

I am so impatient! I want so much for something huge to happen, and I want it *now*! For the past few *decades,* I have felt this sense of anticipation making me feel like something big is around the corner, and we're spinning faster and faster toward it. I think I am afraid I will die before it happens—I'll miss out on it—since I think I have an "expiration date." Yet, it might be so huge, it could possibly scare the heck out of me!

I frequently get the message that right now is a preparation time, and I need to be reading, studying, thinking and gathering information so that down the road, I will have all the knowledge and experience I need to give me the strength to get through the coming events.

This is a "time-out" period for all of us. We are patiently, quietly transforming, and when it is time to step out, we will have shifted into a much higher vibrational level which will make us capable of miraculous deeds. When it is time to come out, the people, places, and opportunities we need to line up with will start to show up. We will be vibrating at a level that attracts others at the same level, and together, we will be able to move mountains.

I can't go from who I am now to who I need to be overnight. That would be overwhelming. I want to open a healing/spiritual center, and even though I know I can have whatever I want, I have had to take a series of baby steps over several years to prepare me for this vision. I have to get a whole list of experiences under my belt before the center can show up. Everything is aligning to prevent a failure.

In all this waiting, it is easy to want to hurry up and make something happen. We get close to stomping our foot to demand this project to be funded *now*. We want to go ahead and quit our job, get that divorce, move to a new area. Yet, I have been reminded by my Guides that we are not to force anything. We need to sit back and patiently wait for the energy to align to bring in what we envisioned. It is not an easy thing to do.

Stay in your high level of enthusiasm and anticipation. You know something big is about to happen. Never give up. Trust what comes every day. It would be so easy to just throw in the towel and think nothing significant is *ever* going to happen. Actually, you are not aware of everything significant that is already happening—a little bit every day. Of course, it is not a little bit. You are on the edge of a huge cliff. When you are willing to trust you are safe, let go and *jump,* knowing you will land where you are needed the most.

So, if you are feeling impatient to "get on with it," just remember you already are getting on with it! You are being guided along the path you need to take to get yourself ready to realize your dream. The people who are to help you are also being guided on the same path that leads to you.

We are on hold, listening to the message, "We thank you for your patience. Someone with be with you shortly." That can also be a message from the Universe! Be patient. Someone *will* be with us shortly!

~~∞∞∞~~

BOTTOM LINE: Play the game in front of you, and when the next game shows up, start playing *that* game.

89

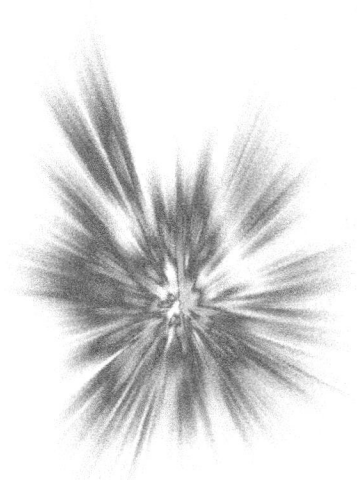

We invite you to order You Already Know This, Vol. I (if you don't already have a copy!) and the You Already Know This—Guidebook at www.OriginalInspirationPublishing.com or on www.amazon.com. Also available on Kindle.

ABOUT THE AUTHOR

Heather M. Clarke is the Founder and Executive Director of the Arizona Enlightenment Center, a gathering place for those on a spiritual path to awakening.

She graduated Arizona State University in 1967 with a Bachelors Degree in Business Administration. She also attended the Southwest Institute of Healing Arts, achieving certifications in Spiritual Studies and Dream Interpretation. She spent over twenty years as a residential real estate agent and she devoted four years to serving as a Red Cross disaster relief volunteer.

She feels that the Arizona Enlightenment Center is her purpose, and she devotes her life to gathering people into a thriving spiritual community at a one-stop shop for good health, wellness, and mind-body-spirit connection–a place where you can live right, eat right, and breathe right.

www.ingramcontent.com/pod-product-compliance
Lightning Source LLC
Chambersburg PA
CBHW060819050426
42449CB00008B/1734